THE *Poetry* REALM

VERSES TO UTOPIA

Vyomini PR Kapse

PARTRIDGE

To order additional copies of this book, contact
Toll Free +65 3165 7531 (Singapore)
Toll Free +60 3 3099 4412 (Malaysia)
orders.singapore@partridgepublishing.com

www.partridgepublishing.com/singapore

Contents

Wonders of Spring... 1

For a Teacher... 2

What is Our Purpose? 3

We are One, We are Strong 4

What is Reality?... 5

There's a Storm A'Coming 7

War: A Scourge to Mankind 9

That House.. 11

I.A.M.. 13

Soldier-God's Angel... 14

#Revive 15

Why Me?.. 16

What If? 19

Them.. 21

Inside Disney 22

The Crisis.. 24

Their Truth 26

Stand Strong... 28

Up There 30

The New Truth.. 32

Our Season 34

I Wish.. 36

Dear 'Man'kind 38

What Matters? 41

Those Days.. 43

Qui êtes vous? 45

The Utopian Dream.. 47

What Do I Do Now? 49

Endless Void... 51

Nothing's Changed... 52

Believe Me?.. 54

Dear Terrans 56

Parallelism.. 58

Lost and Found 59

Ma Meilleure Amie 61

Perfect Imperfections...................................... 63

Remember Me 65

Colours 67

'Her'story... 69

Her.. 70

Rhythm... 71

Queen 72

Apologies? 73

Speechless.. 74

And Consent?.. 75

Paradoxical... 76

Shattered Glass.. 77

Avant Garde 78

Arcady... 79

Poésie 80

Wonders of Spring

I see colourful flowers bloom
As I walk past the Spring Garden opposite my room
Flowers big & small in various hues and shades
& tall grasses with sharp blades

Out in the garden & up in the sky
I gaze at the birds flying high
The sweet songs of birds from their nest
Seems they are ready to welcome a new guest

When I lie on the grass & glare at the sky
I see my granny amidst the clouds & begin to cry
I hear a voice & to my surprise its 'Mother Earth'
She says, "Don't cry dear it's time to mirth.

Our dear guest Spring is on his way,
For all of us to play, swag & be gay."
Ready to go back home after this talk
I was suddenly awoken by a discordant squawk.

For a Teacher

God's most wonderful creation,
Is our teacher.
Our guide to our goals & destination,
Is our teacher.

She taught us what's right & what wrong,
She taught us to always be strong.
She instilled in us morals of values high,
She inspired us to never stop aiming for the sky.

God's most wonderful creation,
Is our teacher.
Our guide to our goals & destination,
Is our teacher.

She is our mother at our second home,
She is our guardian angel in this competitive dome.
She is our moulder & our secrets she bears,
She is the best & beyond compare.

God's most wonderful creation,
Is our teacher.
Our guide to our goals & destination,
Is our teacher.

We would like to take this moment,
To thank you for being our proponent
We would also like to wish for all the joy in the world to you,
P.S. we all truly love you.

What is Our Purpose?

Many a times have I pondered,
What be our purpose,
Many a times have I wondered,
What be our purpose?

Why did God create us,
Why were we crafted,
Was it to cause ruckus,
Was it to cause harm & be shafted?

Why did the Almighty think us to be worthy,
Why did the Supreme one into us breathe life,
Was it to label each other as racists & untrustworthy,
Was it to cause each other pain & strife?

I believe otherwise,
I choose to think differently,
We were fabricated to ensure a tranquil sunrise,
We were invested to better the world to the best of our ability

We are one & have a greater purpose to serve,
We are united & have something to do for this world,
We should pledge to conserve, reserve & preserve,
We should vow to make it a dream world.

We are One, We are Strong

Women's rights are human rights,
You may have suppressed our feelings,
You may have suppressed our voice,
You may have deprived us of our preferences,
You may have deprived us of our rights,
But women's rights are human rights.

Violence against us isn't cultural,
Violence against us is criminal,
Violence against us is pervasive,
Violence against us is pandemic,
We will not be manipulated,
We will not be afflicted.

We want the oppressors prosecuted,
We want the tormentors persecuted,
We want the abusers tyrannized,
We want the bullies victimized,
We want to know we're not alone,
We want to know you've got our back.

We may look feeble but we're strong,
We have the strength to achieve what we desire,
We know equity can't come immediately,
We know it has to be fought for,
That's why we speak with our heads held high,
'Treat us right' cause women's rights are human rights.

What is Reality?

I sit by the window,
Looking at the vast fields,
I sit by the window,
Gazing at the beautiful bields.

I look at the sky,
And see those floss candy like clouds,
I look at the sky,
And see those stars like jewels endowed.

I glimpse at the river,
Flowing with a current tranquil,
I glimpse at the river,
Occasionally running over the jonquil.

I spot a throng of violets,
Ever so beauteous and beguiling,
I spot a throng of violets,
So lovely and alluring.

Far off I descry people on a hill,
Happy couples with their amiable kids,
Far off I descry people on a hill,
Enjoying themselves like no one ever did.

But suddenly I am awoken,
By a thunderclap like sound,
And when my eyes do open,
I am petrified by the sight around.

The vast fields were charred,
They resonated a destruction rooted chord,
The beautiful bields were a graveyard,
They were with dead bodies scarred.

The clouds had turned grey,
They looked like a procession before an affray,
The stars shone dully with dismay,
They displayed humanity's decay.

The river changed colour,
It coruscated with that which is symbolic of valour,
The violets were trampled like sand dollars,
It seemed to be the work of the mauler.

It dawned on me,
That what I had seen,
Was my dreamland's tapestry,
Was nothing but a fantasy.

That this was my life real,
That this was my life's ordeal,
That this was something ideal,
In the life of a refugee girl.

There's a Storm A'Coming

Between the whites and the coloured folks we've differentiated,
Between men and women we've long discriminated,
Here comes a storm fuelled by our distances,
Here comes a storm fuelled by our differences,
Oh! There's a great storm a 'coming.

Towards the victims of sexual abuse we've been stone cold,
Towards the victims of narcotic abuse we've put on a blind fold,
Here comes a storm driven by our ignorance,
Here comes a storm driven by our belligerence,
Oh! There's a great storm a 'coming.

The migrants have been for decades ill-treated,
The refugees for centuries maltreated,
Here comes a storm powered by our vices,
Here comes a storm powered by our offences,
Oh! There's a great storm a 'coming.

Our youth have been enslaved,
Our fledglings have been disenfranchised,
Here comes a storm fired by our irrationality,
Here comes a storm fired by our lunacy,
Oh! There's a great storm a 'coming.

But we can keep this storm at bay,
We can get out of harm's way,
We need only end all our differences,
And prioritize equity over giving men preferences.

We can ward off this storm horrible,
We can avoid this storm terrible,
We must towards victims of abuses develop sympathy,
We ought to help the refugees and imbibe empathy.

It is not too late to save our generation,
It is high time to start looking for a solution,
We must be determined towards our cause and not wuss,
Or else the great storm will be upon us!

War: A Scourge to Mankind

War is not a just way of settling differences
It only deprives us of our rights and preferences
A symptom of man's failure as a thinker is war
Which makes us think whether war is obsolete, or men are
War is the science of destruction
War is organized murder and the innocent's prosecution.

They say war is progress and peace stagnation
But war only results in a nation's devastation
Most of us have been brainwashed and conditioned
But the truth is that war at all costs must be shunned
Since armies are legal, we feel that wars are too
War is nothing but monstrous and that's all that's true

This business of burning people with napalm
Does us so much of harm
They say war is the most significant competition
But it only results in nations attrition
Filling a nation's home with orphans and widows
War is burning of homes and breaking of windows

Fights amongst the various races and creeds
Result in men returning from bloody battle fields
In peace sons bury their fathers
In war the son's ashes the father gathers
War is the time of bloodshed
War is the time of seeing all that red

If we don't end war, it will consume us
For a bad peace or good war there never was
We must end this suffering and strife
We must let our conscience and goodness thrive
We mustn't let this demonic entity of war feed
We must sow the global harmony and peace seed

To end war futile have our efforts been
To not try harder to end it would be a sin
The art of war is so satanic
Our Earth's the rose and war the prick
I just hope to live long enough to see a new era begin
An era in which our Earth with honesty and peace be preened.

That House

In a night as black as coal
This poem of mine untold
This story which on me took its toll
In this very night unfolds

I was moseying down a roan lonely
A road gunyahs chock-a-blocked
When I saw something sui generis remotely
Something cause of which my heart just stopped

No, it was not a sight horrible
No, it was not a mendicant doing his job
It was something for Stalin so veronal
It was a sight that could make Hitler's heart throb

It was not a display of chauvinism ending
It was not an array of our fledgling being uplifted
But it sure was an evince which was fending
A manifestation of something the world has sifted

'Enough of all this suspense', you may say
'Just tell us what you did see'
But promise that you won't dismay
Post I tell you this moment that made me glee

It was but a simple insignificant sight
That is significant in this lost dark world
It was that of one gunyah decorated with lights
That only one along the street with hope burned

That trivial sight illustrated hole reborn
It depicted that there is light in the seas dark
That frivolous sight illuminated a new dawn
It showed that there is of blossoming a spark

Well, you might wonder how this is auxiliary
With the story in this work of literary
Hermano, it teaches us to see light in the darkest of times & to keep hope alive
Sestra, it teaches us to see the good in everything for that is the way to thrive.

J.A.M

We wuss that our lives with problems is loaded,
We crib that we are with cares hoarded,
However there are a handful amongst us,
Who just cannot afford to fuss.

We complain that our country is culpable,
We say it is not worth fighting for, it is deplorable,
But there are a few around here,
Whose thoughts are optimistic and crystal clear.

We feel that there is nothing in our nation to pride,
We are ashamed and our nationality we try to hide,
In our country there are a sporadic scanty,
Who in our enemy's hearts strike bogey.

We overlook that there are people out there,
Who to look death unflinchingly in the eye dare,
We forget that we are the ones at fault,
And that to our anti-patriotism we must put a halt.

The soldiers of our country deserve a tribute to be paid,
A tribute worth more than a thousand words said,
Those who regret that they have but
one life for the nation to give,
Must for eternity in our minds and hearts live.

Soldier-God's Angel

Every night before he goes to sleep
He prays to the Almighty, the Supreme one
To help his handwork's fruit reap
For the sake of his wife, his daughters and sons.

He asks the Lord to bless the day
So that his neighbours struggle not
So that from his brothers and sisters pain is kept away
For they did nothing wrong that this war sought.

But when we think of it that way neither did he
He was but a young man who dreamt
of waving the national flag
One who wanted to do something for the country was he
Alas, it was not meant to be for he was brought home in a bag.

However, he did do something for this glorious nation
He did put his life at stake to safeguard us
He did take three bullets with his face ever so patient
And hence, writing this poem for me was a must.

We must remember those who give their lives for us
We must not sit back and about our petty problems wuss
For this is the story of every soldier out there
Who dies with pride and on his face
a smile of satisfaction wears
This is the tale of the brave men at
Nathula, Wagah and Pulwama
Who die knowing that wrapped around
there would be their Tiranga.

#Revive

We would pray each morning when the Sun rose high,
We would start our day by looking up at the sky.
Then we'd go work for a living,
We'd go work hard and for a square meal keep striving.

Then she came and turned our lives around,
Then she came and changed the whole scenario around.
Buildings rose higher, trees did too,
All of a sudden, everything was devoid of its hues.

People were screaming as they went with the flow,
The world in a split second lost its charm, its glow.
We wondered what sin had we committed?
We wondered hadn't we our everything
to the Lord submitted?

Then why had he set his raging daughter on us?
Why had he asked for the impossible, without any fuss?
We were not the ones who had our Nature fooled,
We respected her, we did not use her like a tool.

Yet, we were the ones who had to pay a heavy price,
Losing everything for someone else's fault was our sacrifice.
All I am saying is that we must to
Nature's distress call pay heed,
Or else the floods would consume you
too-she would make you bleed.

Why Me?

Oh! Just think about the cool breeze
Think about it brushing your face
Oh! Just imagine those tall trees
Imagine them reading to you Heyse

Oh! Just visualize the stream's serene flow
Visualize it carrying you home
Oh! Just envision the hills in dawn's glow
Envision them preaching to you Boehme

Oh! Just envisage the lavender fields
Envisage it embracing your feet as you walk
Oh! Just picture those colourful tulips afield
Picture them singing you to sleep with Bach

How beautiful is our Nature!
But it is destroyed by my crafter
How I wish to see her out of a caricature
And not in a model of before and after

Let us move on to your brethren, dear audience
The new born babies have melted my 'metal' heart
They are teeming with sweetness and obedience
The teenagers, well, they are just down right smart

The adults are lost in a monotonous dimension
It seems they are out to work and for the fledglings earn
The elderly, oh, they just want some attention
All they do is for care and love yearn

These families are a sight to see
But, I, in my whole life have never one seen
These people, I love, sadly-they hate me
Cause I destroy, I am not just evil or mean

I have never gotten to see Nature at its best
I have never had the opportunity to see the youth play
I have never seen Mother Earth's creation rest
For when I arrive, everything turns black and gray

I have seen the breeze halt
I have seen the trees cry
I have seen the streams dry up and gault
I have seen the hills crumble and die

I have seen the lavender fields burn
I have seen the tulips wither
I have seen the tables turn
As people have died hither

I have seen ashes all around
I have heard people scream in pain
I have smelt the air with blood bound
I have felt their hurt, but my sympathy-it's in vain

I have been created to destroy
I have been programmed to attrition
This is my story, it is the tale of a bomb croix
Who never wanted to wreak destruction

If I had it my way, I would law unto myself
If I had it my way, I would never blast
But, alack, I am not the master of myself
Oh! How I wish to let Nature's creation last

This war, this suffering-it all must end
This hate, this bloodshed-it ought to cease
Trust me, my reader, I would do all that it takes to fend
This bomb with an anti-war sentiment pledges to bring peace.

What If?

What if we could all,
Breathe underwater,
Live beyond the burden,
Of man's land lonely,
And from there we could see,
Nature's finest masterpiece,
The lost kingdom of Atlantis?

What if we could all,
Fly so high,
And claim the sky,
Soar above the clouds,
To a place which with hope abounds,
Onwards to our destiny,
To Neverland's fantasy?

What if we could all,
Be ever so bold & brave,
For all family safety's path pave,
Be fearless beyond compare,
To look in the eye the dangers our people bear,
And then could we truly dwell,
And belong in District 12?

What if we could all,
Cultivate relationships strong,
Be able to speak up against things wrong,
A sea of knowledge acquire,

Resource things we do not require,
And the trait of being undaunted share,
To then the title of Divergent bear?

What if we could all,
Escape this world tragic,
By truly making magic,
And conjure spells,
With the wands that shops sell,
Then settle in the wizarding world,
And be a Hogwarts alumni true to word?

What if we could all,
Put our mundane lives in the past,
And learn innumerable runes to last,
And live in harmony,
With the Downworlders we see,
And our bodies paint with marks,
And on a Shadowhunter's journey embark?

Them

The building block of life,
Gets you through all your strifes,
Always stands by your side,
And helps you face the most terrible tide.

A person's support pillar,
The cloud's lining silver,
Every moment has your back,
And never makes you feel that something you lack.

A beautiful musical piece,
Holds all your secret's keys,
Guides you through the darkest nights,
And leads you to the path of light.

Life's most essential necessity,
Know your strengths, your speciality,
Point your flaws out,
But never your potential doubt.

God's marvellous creation,
Love you no matter what the situation,
Bear your worries and struggle for you,
But most importantly care for you too.

They are oxygen to me,
They are a lifeline to me,
They mean the world to me,
Who? Well of course, my family!

Inside Disney

You need not on losing the glass slipper dwell,
Or on the clock striking twelve,
You must have courage and be kind,
For these are the qualities Cinderella teaches us to keep in mind.

You need not to the rose pay heed,
Which loses petals and sows doom's seed,
You must never by the cover judge a book,
For Bella reminds us to in the heart look.

You need not have a face as white as snow,
And to a wicked queen bow,
You must treat equally the big and the small,
For Snow White highlights that we must respect all.

You need not on the spinning wheel ponder,
About pricking your finger and into a death-like-sleep wander,
You must know that into good can evil turn,
As in Aurora's difficulty did love in Maleficent's heart spurn.

Someone cruel may take away your voice,
But like Ariel you must against the odds rise,
One may treat you like a prize to be won,
But like Jasmine you must from your life those people shun.

You may be denied to be a part of the fight,
If so, like Mulan you must pursue the path right,
Some people may try to shatter your dreams,
If so, like Tiana you must with a passion anew teem.

Let no man tell you what you must do,
Like Pocahontas may Nature guide you,
Do not let yourself be traded away for land or power,
Like Merida, embrace the bow and arrow-your power.

They may label you as a threat or naïve,
But like Elsa and Anna you must face them with a heart brave,
They may try to hold you back,
But like Rapunzel you must follow your dreams and not look back.

So all I am trying to say is,
The world of Disney is more than it seems.
Disney is about love, compassion and family,
That is precisely why we will all never be too old for Disney!

The Crisis

I wrote this down to remind us
That the world was once by a crisis gripped
That there was a time when we too did wuss
And like humanity at every stage, once we too stumbled and tripped

Around the world, many fell ill
They fought this battle as deteriorated their health
We lost some, even though they had a strong will
In this one-of-a-kind war they fell, which could not be won by wealth

Several evils shackled our society
As people did not by the law abide
And so grew the casualties and fatality
That were posed by this pandemic spread far and wide

The leaders of the world could not act in time
As they were in the politics entangled
Which made them helpless and mime
And got them in this crisis wrangled

There were those who came to the forefront then
Doctors and nurses to their workplace rushed
And so did the military which serves us through the heat, cold and rain
And they worked during dark nights and mornings hushed

They were pelted by the uncultured
The uncivilized held them back
But from their path away they were not hurled
Their determination caused the miscreants to be taken aback

The condition did worsen
The crisis lasted far too long
But here is a tribute to every person
Who got us through this crisis strong

We shall forever be indebted to you
For your service and selfless sacrifice
In history is a special place reserved for you
For helping us battle this virus shaped vice.

Their Truth

I know a two year old,
To many she may seem to be bold,
But the truth is far more bitter,
For she knows nothing but fear.

I know a seven year old,
Who behaves as though his heart is stone cold,
But in actuality his heart burns,
Cause he for warmth and love yearns.

I know a boy, a teenager,
Who would readily face any danger,
But reality is beyond cruel,
As he is stuck in death's whirlpool.

I know a woman, a mother of two,
To many her life may seem to be of varied hues,
But look closely and one shall see,
She drowns in pain and hurt and is not free.

I know an old couple,
They look as though they live in happiness' bubble,
However that is not the case,
For joy from their lives has been effaced.

This is the story of thousands out there,
No, wait...of millions out there,
Who seem to be alright in this world,
But that is solely cause their voices are not heard.

This is nothing short of doomsday,
This is mankind's decay,
Cause of this many innocent fell,
For this rings our world's death knell.

It does not simply destroy our abode,
It disrupts our life's code,
It is an atrocity which has gone so far,
We must end it, this wicked war.

Stand Strong

You have stained me with your abuses,
You have stained me with these bruises,
How long do you think will I sit silently?
How long do you think will I bear this patiently?

You have wounded me with your insults,
You have wounded me with your assaults,
Do you think I will sit and cower?
Do you think I will drown in fear?

You have me shackled,
You have my heart tethered,
Let me tell you that I will break free,
Oh! Just wait and you shall see.

So what if there aren't more of me at the workplace?
So what if with you we aren't able to 'keep pace'?
Just know that this has been your doing,
Just know that it is you who have us ruined.

So what if there aren't more of me in the army?
So what if you believe that we are 'barmy'?
Let me tell you what will happen now,
For we are no longer going to bow.

You shall see us on the streets storm,
You shall see us for justice swarm,
For equal rights we will stand,
For change we will walk hand-in-hand.

We will rise in these tough times,
For we are not puppets on strings or acts of mime,
We will fight against the odds,
For like you, we too are children of the Lord.

We will battle all the wrongs,
For we are strong,
Our ferocity will leave you smitten,
For we are fearless, we are women.

Up There

The blue and black up there,
With a splash of purple and white,
From where we are down here,
Is nothing short of a beauteous sight.

But I often wonder,
What lies in that vast expanse,
I sit and ponder,
Over the sight which has left me in a trance.

The clusters of cotton candy like,
Fluffy white clouds,
Which in my heart and mind strike,
A vision of heaven's court all around.

The sparkling studs,
Embedded in the sky,
The twinkling diamonds,
That dance when I close my eyes.

The gleaming shooting stars,
Leave a trail of pixie dust like mist,
And though they seem to be afar,
Shall fulfil my heart's desire in a second's gist.

She said she was going to utopia,
I deliberate over where she went,
She said she was moving on to the Numen's arena,
Unknown to her whereabouts-I sit and lament.

But when I look up at the ether,
I feel ever so reassured,
When I sit and stare into the azure,
I sense her presence, I feel secured.

For when I glimpse at the paradise,
The clouds form her calm face,
The stars her patient smile,
And I am then by my Grandma embraced.

So what truly lies in the Elysian Fields?
What are its treasure-yet to be unveiled?
Dear readers, the welkin but holds,
That which we lost-one we can no longer hold.

The New Truth

That five year old,
Who lives in the slums,
Knows nothing but cold,
So at the sight of the Sun he jumps.
His hands know only the cane,
And his mind the pain,
For he knows not that something,
Which could spare him from to this future succumbing.

That seven year old,
From that tumble down shack,
Has heard several tales told,
About a time of prosperity from long back.
A time when every fledgling,
Had food to eat and clean water to drink,
But misfortune over this little girl's head hails,
For she can only satisfy her hunger by listening to these tales.

That eleven year old boy,
Who from his native country has been displaced,
Due to the war that his home did destroy,
Is by the sight of sky-high towers fazed.
But the rich knew not sympathy,
Towards his loss none displayed empathy,
So he sits on the footpath with a picture of his family,
Wondering what could save him from his tyrannical destiny.

That fifteen year old girl,
With the biggest smile in school,
Has been misused and hurled,
Into shame and agony's whirlpool.
A victim of the most heinous crime,
Waited for justice for a protracted time,
But the malefactors still roam free,
Because no one stood up for this patsy.

We must help these children,
We must rush to aid the youth,
We must ensure and make certain,
That they know their new truth.
They will no longer be deprived,
They will no longer be shackled,
They will be given their rights,
So that they can reach new heights.

Our Season

It is that time of the year,
When the rustling of leaves we hear,
And as the orange-red leaves fall,
A tale untold I recall.

Every autumn, my father and I,
Would play in heaps of leaves high,
We would stand by the lake,
Gazing at all the beauty we could take.

Next year, he decided to stay home,
So I brought autumn to our humble dome,
As on the soft white bed he lay,
I placed those beauteous leaves at bay.

A few more autumns passed,
And to the last few years contrast,
My father sat on a berth in a city far,
Looking out the window at the innumerable stars.

And I sat in our little hometown,
On a wooden bench looking around,
That year the tree shed its leaves the most,
And tears stained my cheeks as I sat at my post.

Somehow we both knew when,
And we closed our eyes then,
He could see the golden-orange with a hint of red,
I could see the blue-black with sparkling studs instead.

We saw one another too,
For the last time-we knew,
He hoped that I will soon be at ease,
And I hoped that he truly finds peace.

Ten years have now gone by,
And every time that I close my eyes,
I am taken back to our autumn,
When I was a little girl and he and I were one.

I Wish

I wish-people stop judging me,
For who I am and who I want to be.
They think twice before using me like a tool,
For I am not an afraid and a suppressed fool.
They treat me right and not withhold what I deserve,
For I am no longer by their threats unnerved.
I wish-imbibing reverence for a woman is made a custom,
I wish to be untied from this shallow society, I wish for freedom!

I wish-these folks understand my situation,
For I am a victim of colossal discrimination.
They impasse their display of racism,
For I refuse to be silenced and hit rock bottom.
They grant me my liberties and rights,
For, much like them, it is my birth right.
I wish-slogans a reality in the near future become,
I wish black lives do matter, I wish for freedom!

I wish-the populace accepts me,
Even though I belong to the 'rainbow community'.
They empower me to learn and pursue my vocation,
Even though in their eyes I might be a 'mutation'.
They concede my right basic and fundamental,
Even though when it comes to love my heart is 'fickle'.
I wish-Article 377 becomes a worldwide obiter dictum,
I wish to be regarded with equity, I wish for freedom!

I wish-this community welcomes me,
Although, I am of a different nationality.
They proffer me a shelter and the basic necessities,
Although in their opinion, I hail from the 'land of mutinies'.
They display compassion, goodwill and empathize,
Although, I am another country's member disenfranchised.
I wish-refugees no longer be dubbed as the problem,
I wish for a new and better life, I wish for freedom!

I wish-the masses comprehend my pain,
For I have been enchained, maimed and restrained.
They unravel that this issue is not facetious,
For it breaks the innocent, this matter is odious.
They take to the streets to express their dissent,
For I am no longer willing to sit back and lament.
I wish-the patsies of abuses no more need succumb,
I wish to feel protected and safe, I wish for freedom!

We all wish to be unshackled,
From the chain-like vices that grip our society.
We all desire to be respected,
No matter what be our identity.
We all crave to be treated as equals,
For we were never created as disparate mortals.
We all yearn for that solitary opportunity,
To be heard and just break free!

Dear 'Man'kind

Broken and shattered
Are the glass shards
Which have my body marred
And my heart scarred

Crooked and twisted
Are the metal pieces w
Which have my back pierced
And my mind with pain versed

I am crying, I am hurting
My eyes are resonating agony
I am bleeding, I am struggling
My ears are amplifying this cacophony

Help me-I'm drowning
In this dark sea of hopelessness
Save me-I am dying
In this lost world that is now a mess

That cane-thin, but gashing
I can still hear it lashing
Against my gentle, soft skin tender
Forcing me to then surrender

That spot-in that lone ghost town
Where I was brutally pinned down
Despite my vehement fulminations
Thus rendering me futile during that predation

I am aching as I am facing
My last few days alone
I am anguishing as I am bandaging
With time the wounds that have but grown

Save my skin-I mean it literally
For I no longer recognize the one in the mirror
Succour me-from this villainy
For my end is inching ever to nearer

I cannot speak, I cannot talk
Though, do not mistake my silence for fear
I am impeded by my tongue speared
Whilst I am with Death at cross walks

I cannot move, I am motionless
But, do not misinterpret my immobility
I am prevented by my castrated disability
Whilst my breath I lose and become restless

I know now what my future holds
I know now what lies at the end of this road
For my mind with pain will continue to reel
For these bruises and wounds will never heal

I was exploited and illtreated
Made a victim of the most heinous crime
I was mauled and molested
Inflicted horrors upon, maimed and mimed

Now as I Mosey along to
Embrace dear old Death
I whisper under my breath
'Dear 'man'kind this one thing you must do.

Spare the others that you
Planned on roping into this spiteful hap.'
And as Death around me his arms wraps
I hope that my wish comes true.

What Matters?

His moist eyes search
For a soul kind
Outside the deserted church
To free him from the binds
Of hunger, thirst, heat, cold and pain,
Whilst in shredded garments he faces the rain.

Her throat parched calls
For a munificent ka
Along the lone street that she sprawls
To unfetter her from the claw
Of torment and trauma, anguish and agony
As with bruises and wounds she faces this fatality.

His blaring ears patiently discern
For a pneuma generous
Near the river stagnant and fields burnt
To unchain him from the shackles venomous
Of massacre, slaughter, quietus and horror
Whilst with his body maimed, he faces this torture.

Her stoic face knocks on every door
For a compassionate spirit
In the but beauteous city of a lore
To unbound her from the vile pivot
Of abhorrence, prejudice, spite and hate
As in circles of ostracism she waits.

His mother yearns for a benignant
Her father asks for a heart tender
Their grandparents want an indulgent
Our child gazes for one who cares.

The fledgling seated in the wheelchair
Desires love and affection
The autistic we met on the stairs
Wishes for grace and protection.

The helpers and workers
Crave for one generous and giving
The rainbow tribe standing in corners
Long for a being magnanimous and feeling.
This dark world is lost
In a sea of misery and despair
But if of kindness we build crofts
We can guide it elsewhere.

Those Days

I remember the aesthetic sight
Of the snow being rolled into
Perfect-imperfect balls white
And being embedded into.
There are fresh carrots and beady eyes
And twigs along with a scarf or tie
To create a snowman before daybreak
The ideal Winter Playmate.

I remember the fragrance
Of the freshly baked gingerbread
The delicious turkey and bacon
To keep us for eternity fed.
With plum cakes under the mistletoe
And apple pies under the tree's star's glow
To celebrate yet another New Year's Eve
During this season in which we for joy believe.

I remember the bland taste
Which tingled my tongue
As I the path traced
Where I oft on the swing swung
And the road which was lined
With hailstones and crystals fine
To announce-'My beloved people
Your dear friend Winter is one his way, surreal!

I remember the sound
Of children's gay laughter
In somewhat of a melody bound

With the merry Christmas carols
And the tune ever so pleasing
Of kids in the soft snow playing
To enjoy to the fullest this
Experience of heaven's bliss.

But it is December now
And my friends tell me
Nothing is the same now
And my family tells me
This Winter will not be
Like the ones before
For everything by this pandemic
Has been shaken to the core.

Now as I sit and stare
Into the infinite azure
My mind begins to wander
As I yet again ponder
We are with our loved ones
During this hopeful and joyous season
We are safe and sound
And the never seen wonders know no bound.

The celebrations though abated
Have not been halted
The feast though truncated
Has not been abandoned
The carols though diminished
Have not vanished
And our love despite our barriers
Has never been so strong and superior.

Qui êtes vous?

C'est la vie mais
It is 'the' life but
Ce n'est pas votre destin
It is not your destiny
Soyez courageux et combattez
Have courage and fight
Tous les obstacles et problèmes
All the obstacles and problems
Car tu es forte
For you are strong
Car tu es une femme
For you are a woman
Car tu es prête
For you are poised
Car tu es une femme
For you are a woman
Mais vous êtes aussi gentil
But you are also kind
Mais vous êtes aussi douce
But you are also sweet
Mais vous vous souciez aussi
But you also care
Mais vous aimez aussi
But you also love
Et tu es féroce
And you are ferocious
Et tu es une femme
And you are a woman
Et vous êtes une fille, une mère
And you a daughter, a mother

Et vous êtes une amie, une sœur
And you are a friend, a sister
Vous êtes respecté et
You are respected and
Vous êtes le monde pour certains
You are the world for some
Alors garde la tête haute
So hold your head high
Car tu es une femme.
For you are a woman.

The Utopian Dream

My head just reels,
Because I know how that young girl feels,
To be told 'you don't belong',
To be told 'you are always wrong',
To be told 'never were you wished for by our kith',
To be told 'you will always be a misfit',
And to walk away with a smile,
As that's just how it's been for a while.

My eyes just truly pain,
Watching that teenage girl run around in vain,
Trying to fit in with the elite crowd,
Only to find her voice subdued by those people loud,
Trying to hide her hideous scars,
And lock her true self in a place far,
Trying to cover up all the flaws,
So that she is deemed worthy by society's laws.

My ears screen the sound,
When I hear tales of the lady bound,
Locked away in a room dark,
So that no one can see her potential's spark,
Dissevered by the oppugners in ways unimaginable,
To earn off the streets and save them the trouble,
And then sold to a man unknown,
Who hurls her into a state of being torn.

My heart breaks and it aches,
For the woman who puts everything at stake,
Only to be disrespected for her position,
Only to be denied her well-deserved promotion,
Only to be ridiculed for sitting at home,
Only to be treated as a liability in her own dome,
And what be the reason?
That she is a girl, a lady, a woman!

Trust me-sexism is a bane,
And chauvinism is just another pain,
Misogyny should be side-lined,
And toxic femininity must be to the past confined,
These are the vices which shackle our world,
These are the sins which restrain mankind.

I say, treat us women with respect,
I say, treat us right,
Support us in life's every aspect,
Support us to have a future bright,
So, join hands now and take the pledge,
For feminism is about equity, we don't have no grudge

What Do I Do Now?

My Mama told me,
The day you bleed,
You have grown,
To be a woman now.

My Mama told me,
Do not pay heed,
To the hate seeds sown,
And the cold hearted vows.

But how can I ignore,
The spiteful glances they cast,
When the blood is displaced,
From its original path?

But how can I ignore,
The murmurs that last,
In the place holy and chaste,
Where incurred upon me are wraths?

My Mama told me,
That my body is transforming,
Into a temple to carry,
A little numen in the future.

My Mama told me,
That the crowd's swarming,
May speak things unnecessary,
And try to tear up the sutures.

But how can I ignore,
That uncomfortable feeling,
I experience for five days,
Every single month?

But how can I ignore,
This pain freewheeling,
These cramps which my mind haze,
As these men snicker every time I grunt?

But my Mama taught me,
To always be happy,
To respect my body,
For I, a goddess embody.

And my Mama taught me,
To care for my health,
Look after myself,
And to not forget to love myself!

Endless Void

I am falling – endlessly,
I cannot see what is around me,
I can but feel,
The wind bitter and chill,
I can only hear,
The screeching sounds in fear,
I can but smell,
The rotting odour of Hell,
I can only taste,
The air teeming with bitter haste,
I do not know how,
I can save myself now.

But as my eyes do prance,
To upon a beam of hope chance,
They are greeted by a glimmer,
Of faith like light which does shimmer,
And I slowly then comprehend,
That I am not inching towards the end,
And with a heart so steady,
I am but ready,
To in this abyss helter-skelter pace,
For I know, I shall slip into the Lord's warm embrace.

Nothing's Changed

"Little one, what are you doing
Sitting here for long hours?"
In a voice melodious and chiming
The next door neighbour inquires
"This festive season is unlike
The ones from quite some time before
Then from where does your mirth derive?"
She questions in the tone of a lore.

"Auntie, my father has returned
From a lone ghost town
Where his heart yearned
For five long years, to come back around
No longer is he engrossed
In his eternally tedious work
And no longer is my mother crossed
For having to single handedly manage all the work."

"Yesterday, as we drove past
The streets teeming with a glow anew
Our glances were thence cast
At the people and houses in our view
Every person seemed to cherish
During these times, moments of togetherness
Every dome seemed to relish
The season of love and joy in these times messed."

"How then is this festive season
Different from its forerunners
When compassion and hope for one
Are during this crisis, its wonders?
Auntie, why do you not try and
Embrace the happiness this season brings
I know you have troubles and cares at hand
But let this season be your wings."

She glanced at me for quite some time
Before opening the door
And with a look solemn and mime
She knelt beside me on the floor
As I looked at her then
A slow smile dawned upon my face
For she said- "Nothing has truly changed
So let us this time together celebrate!"

Believe Me?

I know not what I did wrong for
There are now shards of glass
In places they must not be
There are scraps of metal
Which make me bleed
There are cuts & wounds
Which deepen over time
And there are bruises and scars
That may never heal
And every man & woman
Walking down this gloomy street
Whisper my name with
Deep rooted hatred & shame
They must think I am to blame
For speaking out loud and
Never submitting to the elite & proud
They must think I am at fault
For my grief & sorrow & pain
For all the events transpired but
I believe definitely not!

But what does it matter
What I think & what I believe
Whether I am a few days later
Able to survive, able to live
But I will no longer
Sit & in fear cower
I will not be silenced
By the multitude of commoners
I will not be forced

Into a void of shame & self-hate
I will speak out loud
And let my heart be voiced out
I will not be the victim
I will be the warrior and
I will bring about a change
For now my soul is enraged
So do not infuriate my modesty
For now I shall write my own Odyssey!

Dear Terrans

I am aware that my methods,
Were improper and miscalculated,
I am aware that my decisions,
Were untimely and misjudged.

But I do hope that for all,
The troubles I caused you,
But I do hope that for all,
This pain you went through.

You understand what,
I was trying to say,
You comprehend,
My impetus, my purpose.

I believe you now grasp,
The importance of a family,
I believe you now grasp,
That little things matter.

I trust you discern,
That one can make do,
I trust you discern,
That joy is measured by what we have.

I consider that you have,
Learned to embrace challenges,
I consider that you have,
Made the best of this 'new normal'.

I feel that my work here,
Is hence done,
I feel that I must,
Leave you to be.

I must reiterate however,
Before we our ways part,
I must reiterate however,
That my strategy was erroneous.

But the lessons that you have acquired,
And the knowledge that you have gained,
Carry it along with you forever as you enter,
A new season, a new year, a new beginning.

Best Regards,
COVID-19.

Parallelism

I envisage
An alternate universe
Where relationships thrive
On love sans divide
Where families last
On trust sans divide

I envisage
An alternate universe
Where weapons like
Dust away fleet
Where wars like
Bad memories away fleet

I envisage
An alternate universe
Where caste is but
A word seated idly
Where sexuality is but
A term moseying idly

I envisage
An alternate universe
A parallel world
Which mirrors this reality
To the utopian realm
Which I wish to call home!

Lost and Found

I have wandered,
These lonely streets,
I have meandered,
These dark seas,
Wondering where,
I truly did belong,
Pondering over when,
I would groove to that love song.

I have knocked,
On every emotionless door,
I have asked,
These shallow eyes for more,
For I always knew,
What I did deserve,
But never knew,
Where a seat for me was forever reserved.

I have cried and wept,
For the now strangers,
I have my heart broken had,
For my now paradoxically blank canvas,
But as I am now resigned,
In this distant ghost town,
A thought clouds my mind,
And it truly does with my feelings resound.

All that I ever wanted,
All that I ever needed,
All that I ever desired,

All that fuels my heart's fire,
Was always there for me to confide,
Was always there by my side,
Was always there to guide me right,
Was always there to hold me tight.

And now as I head back,
To a place I have forever known,
I hope you do not hold back,
And accept me for the one I have into grown,
For you are my unique celestial being,
And my love for you knows no bounds,
So let us a new chapter together begin,
For I was lost, but with you I am found.

Ma Meilleure Amie

Que faut-elle,
What does it take,
Pour être une bonne amie?
To be a good friend?
Que faut-elle,
What does it take,
Pour rester avec quelqu'un jusqu'à la fin?
To stand with someone till the end?

Un cœur d'or,
A heart of gold,
Une âme si audacieuse.
A soul so bold.
Des yeux pleins de détermination,
Eyes teeming with determination,
Des yeux apaisant ses hésitations.
Eyes easing one's hesitation.

Une personne qui vous fait,
A person who makes you,
Se sentir bien dans sa peau.
Feel good in your own skin.
Une personne qui vous fait,
A person who makes you,
Sentir aimé et comme un semblable.
Feel loved and as one akin.

Celui qui, tard dans la nuit,
One who at late nights,
Est là pour vous parler patiemment.
Is there to talk with you patiently.
Celui qui, à la fin de la nuit,
One who at late nights,
Est là pour vous faire sentir plein d'espoir et prêt.
Is there to make you feel hopeful and ready.

Une humaine que peut porter,
A human who the title,
Le titre de votre sœur,
Of your sister may bear.
C'est elle qui restera,
She is the one who will,
Là jusqu'à la fin pour vous.
Till the end, for you be there.

Perfect Imperfections

Our love was not
Black and white for
It had its ups and downs and what not
But we made it this far.

Our love was not
What one may refer to
As a love so perfect
But we were together-meant to.

And so we got through
The tides of insecurities
The storms of jealousy
The dusk of fights
And the buts, ifs and mights.

This love of varied hues
Did for eternity survive
And our love still thrives
Every time we vows exchange
And say sweet phrases in the day's range.

Our love shall only grow
For the years to come, for infinity
And everything that life at us throws
Shall be by our solidity
Dodged and passed for
We have celebrated our flaws.

We are strong as hellfire
In this world with angels wired
For the girl in the mirror
And I, have never been braver
Our secret-Well we have but
The power of self-love learnt!

Remember Me

One fault of mine
Or rather one step
Which I believed was then fine
Now in my heart has it crept
For I know now what you always meant to me
For I comprehend now we were meant to be
They say time heals one's scars
They say time heals your pain
But what if it was your heart that was marred
Will we ever be the same?
I wish I could reach out to you
Every time that I cried
But I was aware of what I did to you
And my feelings I did try to hide
My decisions were horribly wrong
And I am reminded of that by every song
But I wish I could now change
Our present and future for that's in our range
I do not wish to let you go
But every second am I now haunted by this thought
For I just cannot let you go
But I do not believe you will trust my thoughts
Just know that I do wish the best for you
And that I shall forever be there for you
But I am afraid for I have broken you one time
But I hope you think of me yet another time
One fault of mine and we went

From something we knew to something we do not
If only I could make you see
The change that this time has brought in me
I love you and I know you know
But there is only one hope which in my heart is sowed
I hope that when you are ready
Just once please do remember me.

Colours

Black,
The colour of her eyes,
The marks on her back and thighs,
From the torture she was subjected to,
From the lash which her skin did give this hue.

Blue,
The colour of her arms,
The blows which on her body were dawned,
From the abuse she was made a victim of,
Despite her 'no' which was shadowed by their scoffs.

Red,
The colour of her scars,
The wounds which her skin mar,
From the brutality she has faced,
And the torment which her feelings did efface.

Grey,
The colour of her world,
The place where she is unheard,
For her voice here deserves no place,
And her standing here has no space.

White,
The colour of her salt sprinkled tears,
Which through her eyes spear,
The moment she experiences excruciating pain,
Or the moment she realizes her struggle is in vain.

Yellow,
The colour of the sun whose warmth her skin never knew.
Orange,
The colour of the sunrise and sunset which to her may seem anew.

Pink,
The colour of the roses which never mingled with her hair.
Purple,
The colour of the violets at which she never got to stare.

Green,
The colour of the vast fields she never meandered.
Golden,
The colour of the beauteous beaches she never wandered.

Brown,
The colour of the mud her feet have never felt.
Silver,
The colour of the shells amongst which she has never knelt.

As her beauteous eyelids try to shield,
Her from the dystopia afield,
She realizes the colours which,
Her life, her reality do stitch,
And she slowly does begin to comprehend,
Her colour blindness has from her agony stemmed,
But she whispers to herself in a voice hushed and low,
'You are beautiful' and that is all your eyes shall know.

'Her'story

'And I ask but one thing from you,'
Said Mumtaz Mahal in a voice,
So comely and with a gaze true,
'So that you are never of me devoid,
Build me a marvel where I may reside,
Once I leave the mortal realm behind,
And let it be but an emblem of,
Pure love sans barriers and divide,
And let it be but a symbol of,
Two hearts which shall forever be aligned.'
'Oh, my dearest Mumtaz! Why is it that,
You utter the words I wish you never had.
Why do you speak of parting ways,
When I am but prepared to set ablaze,
This wonted universe for your fine fettle?'
Then with a heart heavy began the
making of something special.

Her

Dear Mother,
You taught me the meaning of life,
You taught me to adorn a spectrum of hats,
You were a mother, a daughter and a wife,
You were the one who held the maps,
To every ambition shaped dream like road,
And as you assumed the likes of a guiding light,
And the lineaments of everything right,
Did I something then decode,
You were but my best friend, not an enemy,
You were but my beacon of hope, not a paradoxical entity,
You have moulded me into the woman I have become,
You have imbibed in me compassion and love's strum,
You have endowed me with the lessons of self-love,
You have edified me with familial love being over and above,
They say it is better late than never,
And while I know that we have forever,
I have often afeared not having a chance,
To look at you with a gratifying glance,
And as the steady riverlike flowing tears do stain my cheeks,
I shall but thank you for I have no other phrase to speak.

Rhythm

Lub Dub
Dub Lub
Two hearts beating,
With different rhythms,
Could you see the love fleeting?
Could you feel the music lissom?

And as the distance comes creeping,
Two hearts are but aching,
Two souls are but bleeding,
As their eyes are but the other seeking.

Lub Dub
Lub Dub
Two hearts beating,
With an ever so synchronous rhythm,
Could you see the love gradually breeding?
Could you feel the harmonies arisen?

And as the spaces in between are fading,
Two hearts are but blazing,
Two souls are but awakening,
As their eyes are no longer pacing.

Queen

I do not need to,
The multitude's cries garner,
I do not need no,
Knight in shining armour,
I do not need to,
Ride a horse with my head held high,
I do not need no,
Weapons to on the seemingly 'weak' unjustly pry,
I do not need no,
Men to 'guide' my thoughts helter,
I do not need no,
Men to make me 'bite' my tongue skelter,
For the centuries of oppression,
And for these decades of discrimination,
Have taught me my place,
And who I have forever been,
And with my thoughts have I come at pace,
That I have always been but a queen.

Apologies?

Dear Humans,
Forgive me for failing you
And your insatiable desires
Forgive me for failing you
And your race's ravenous desires

But wasn't my brother's ivory enough?
Wasn't my sister's horn enough?
Didn't my neighbour's skin and scales suffice?
Didn't my friend's body suffice?

But I must apologise and exalt
For I have come to realise
My brethren were never at fault
Your hearts do hate and lies comprise.
~The star crossed animal kingdom

Speechless

My mom is the happiest when
She is assured that her little girl
Has been safeguarded by the numen
And has escaped the terror bound whirl
Which has this nation since
Tumultuous decades flung into an abyss
And when I am but out of her
Honey like patient eyes' sight
Do the tears of joy begin to appear
For her selfless heart does sense the light
To save but me from this endless void
And though she is of the hope devoid
To persevere and this storm brave
She is happy for she knows her fledgling is safe.

And Consent?

The clothes she wore,
The look in her eyes,
The smile she wore,
Caught your light eyes,
But why did your ears
Not hear the sound,
Of the whispers
Which did a NO resound?

Paradoxical

Envisage this
An alternate universe
In the phase of the 13th century
Where fairies administer
The working of the commonwealth
Where witches run
The business houses
Where goblins and gnomes ensure
That every creature has enough
resources to sustain themselves
Where centaurs and unicorns fight
In the armies which have never been to war
For this universe knows but peace
And where mermaids guard and protect
The boundaries of this commonwealth
Which knows not what the future holds
And dwells in blissful ignorance
Of the dawn of the era of Adam and Eve.

Shattered Glass

Why is it that Nefertiti
Is the Great Royal Wife labelled?
Why is it that Nefertiti
Was merely used as an heir bearer?
But let us thank Cleopatra
For showing us that,
'A queen without her king
Historically speaking, is more powerful'!
History has highlighted the need
To shatter the existing patriarchal structures,
So let us all lead like a feminist
For 'ce n'est pas la vie, c'est ta vie'!

Avant Garde

May we live to
See the dawn of an era
Where she makes heads bow and not turn
May we live to
See the dawn of an era
Where she is not interrupted
May we live to
See the dawn of an era
Where she is empowered and respected
May we live to
See the dawn of an era
Where the future lies in the hands of women!

Arcady

May we reach this stage
Where written on every page
Will be that it is absolutely fine
For boys to cry and whine
And express their emotions
Where written on every page
Will be that is it absolutely essential
For girls to be treated in not a direction tangential
And be able to voice their opinions.

Poésie

My heart bleeds on these papers,
My soul aches on these parchments,
My ink blots sorrow on these papers,
My words resound emotions on these parchments,
A few pages interspersed with,
Thoughts never before voiced,
A few lines interspersed with,
Words never before voiced,
Unfelt emotions and unheard words,
Unthought thoughts and unsaid words,
But the recto and verso in my hand,
Dance with the joys of my heart,
Mourn with the griefs of my soul,
Smirk with my thoughts sarcastic and,
Resonate and resound all I feel,
All I think and all I wish to speak,
For these poems are but my window,
To a utopia whose part I wish to be.

CPSIA information can be obtained
at www.ICGtesting.com
Printed in the USA
LVHW032229250521
688475LV00005B/237